Popular Dog Library

Cocker Spaniel

Michael Teasley

Published in association with T.F.H. Publications, Inc.,
the world's largest and most respected publisher of pet literature

Chelsea House Publishers
Philadelphia

CONTENTS

Cocker Spaniel History 1
Description of the Breed 4
A Cocker in the Family 6
Standard for the Breed 9
Cocker Spaniel Grooming 19
The Sporting Cocker 25
Your Cocker's Health 33
Feeding 39
Training 49
Your New Cocker Spaniel Puppy 53
Showing A Cocker Spaniel 61

Popular Dog Library

Labrador Retriever
Rottweiler
German Shepherd
Golden Retriever
Poodle
Beagle
Dachshund
Cocker Spaniel
Yorkshire Terrier
Pomeranian
Shih Tzu
Chihuahua

Publisher's Note: All of the photographs in this book have been coated with FOTO-GLAZE® finish, a special lamination that imparts a new dimension of colorful gloss to the photographs.

Reinforced Library Binding & Super-Highest Quality Boards

This edition © 1995 TFH Publications, Inc., 1 TFH Plaza, Neptune City, NJ 07753. This special library bound edition is made expressly for Chelsea House Publishers, a division of Main Line Book Company.

Library of Congress Cataloging-in-Publication Data

Teasley, Michael.
Guide to owning a cocker spaniel / by Michael Teasley.
    p.   cm. — (Popular dog library)
Originally published: Neptune City, N.J. : T.F.H. Publications, c1995.
Includes index.
Summary: Discusses choosing a cocker spaniel, the history of the breed, puppy care, grooming, training, and more.
ISDN 0-7910-5477-2 (hc)
1. Cocker spaniels Juvenile literature.   [1. Cocker spaniels. 2. Dogs. 3. Pets.]
I. Title. II. Series.
SF429.C55T425   1999
636.752'4—dc21   99-15131
                                                                            CIP

COCKER SPANIEL HISTORY

No one knows the beginnings of the close association between humans and dogs, but the relationship must have extended thousands of years prior to our earliest records. The most ancient of the sculptures and bas-reliefs, more frequently than not, show a dog in the scene. From that beginning the canine family has developed and produced so many true-to-type families that the American Kennel Club now recognizes well over 100 separate breeds. There are also several breeds not recognized by that club.

Many of the dog breeds of today are "manufactured" breeds. Man, visualizing in his mind's eye his ideal dog to suit a given purpose, proceeded to interbreed two or more distinct breeds or types until in the progeny he found a pair that fit his picture. As succeeding progeny more closely approached the end sought, the lesser specimens were culled out and the better ones bred until finally the planned breed, with type firmly fixed, resulted. Within an already established breed, if a breeder wanted to increase the size of his dogs, for instance, he would select and breed only the larger specimens.

THE SPANIEL FAMILY

Spaniels comprise a very old dog family. No one knows for sure when or where they originated. Spaniels are mentioned in writings of the 14th century, and that's far enough back for this writer. They are commonly supposed to have been a Spanish family, although several early Spaniels were found in Switzerland and France. The earliest drawings available make them look more like a "ratty" setter than a spaniel; taller and rangier, with a full-length tail carrying something of a flag and with comparatively short ears.

As civilization progressed and people became intrigued with the idea of producing "man made" breeds, Spaniels were taken across Europe and into the hands of breeders in England; most of the separation of the general Spaniel family into many separate and distinct breeds originated there. Today there are such distinct Spaniel breeds as the American Water, Brittany, Clumber, Cocker, English Cocker, English Springer, Field, Irish Water, Sussex, and Welsh Springer.

In the early days of attaching

PHOTO BY ISABELLE FRANCAIS.

The Cocker Spaniel is part of the family of hunting dogs that has been in existence as far back as the 14th century.

Despite very close ties to the American version, the English Cocker Spaniel is considered a separate breed and interbreeding between the two is forbidden.

subtitles to the Spaniels, it was common practice to have Cockers, Springers, etc., come out of a single litter, the only difference being size. Then as dog shows came into being and refinements were bred into the various strains, the prefixes stuck, and breed by breed the individual Spaniels came to be separated from the whole family. It was not until 1883 that Cockers were given their own classification in the shows, and ten years later they were recognized as a distinct breed in the English stud book.

COCKERS IN THE UNITED STATES

It was sometime in the 1880s that the first Cockers came to the United States, and the famous Obo dogs set the pattern for what is now known in the United States as the Cocker Spaniel. It should be noted here that this version of the breed is called the American Cocker Spaniel by British dog fanciers. It also should be noted that a breed known as the Cocker Spaniel in Great Britain is called the English Cocker Spaniel by Americans.

Years ago, when Americans were importing many Cockers from England, both American and English Cockers were entered indiscriminately in the dog shows as Cocker Spaniels. A breeder could take his choice and enter one dog from a litter as an English Cocker and another from the same litter as an American Cocker. Now they are separate and distinct breeds, and interbreeding is forbidden.

It was in 1920 that Red Brucie

arrived on the scene, and the Cocker started his complete change in appearance. He came along at just the right time, and, being a very prepotent dog, really gave Cockers a "new look": up on leg, shorter in the back, with a longer neck sloping into trim, tight shoulders. Not a champion himself, he nevertheless set an all-breed record for his time by siring 38 champions.

The American Cocker Spaniel has evolved into a much different breed from its English cousin. This American Cocker exhibits the main characteristic differences from the English Cocker: shorter snout, greater height, shorter back, more abundant coat and feathering, and a longer neck that slopes onto trim, tight shoulders.

DESCRIPTION OF THE BREED

Originally, the Cocker Spaniel was a gun dog, developed and used mainly in England on upland game; hence his designation as a "Cocking" Spaniel, later to be contracted to "Cocker." This bit of history ties in with character, because gun dogs must be of a high degree of intelligence and readily trainable, possessed of an aggressive yet steady temperament.

That, indeed, is a good description of the character of the Cocker Spaniel—happy, very bright, loyal, and understanding of his master's moods or the task of the moment. His size, physical beauty, and temperament soon attracted wide attention as the ideal family companion. As time passed, the Cocker came to be accepted for that place in the canine picture, and his use in the field became more and more infrequent. We must bear in mind in that connection that up until about 1925 Cockers were much smaller than they are today, and much longer in the back than they were high at the shoulder. So it is not to be wondered at that the early Cockers, though they had the nose and the heart for field work (and loved it) would be passed by in favor of their big

PHOTO BY ISABELLE FRANCAIS.

Originally developed as a gun dog, the Cocker Spaniel has won over the hearts of many as a house pet for the same reasons he was loved by hunters: intelligence, loyalty, happiness, and steady temperament.

The Cocker's convenient size and irresistible disposition have made him an ideal family companion.

brothers, the Springers and the other sporting Spaniel breeds.

AN ADAPTABLE GUN DOG

In more recent years, with Cockers of 35 pounds the rule rather than the exception, and with body proportions brought into balance so that today they are about as high at the shoulder as they are long in back, there has been quite a resurgence in field trial activity. With a very serious-minded group determined to re-establish the Cocker's place among the gun dogs, considerable headway is being made in that direction. The fact remains that it is his adaptability as the family

companion that has made him so popular.

Let's keep in mind, however, the fact that the Cocker is primarily a gun dog—not a lap dog, and not a toy. It is the Cocker's in-between size plus his irresistible disposition that is responsible for his popularity as the family companion. He is small enough so that he creates no domestic housing problem and can live in the home with the family without special arrangements having to be made for him. On the other hand, he is large enough to be rugged, well able to take weather, and definitely not a toy to be bundled up when he goes out into the cold.

A COCKER IN THE FAMILY

The Cocker Spaniel is a wonderful children's dog and loves to romp with them. On the other hand, he is equally exuberant and happy tramping the woods and fields with the master of the household, busily smelling out the gamy scents his keen nose detects.

The Cocker adapts to most environments, and thousands of them spend their lives in super-heated apartments, always taken out on a leash and never enjoying the slightest freedom to follow their natural instincts. The reason that the Cocker is so adaptable is that primarily he is happy just to be close to his family, but that does not mean that family life finds him at his best or that he is completely happy in it. Rather, he settles into a life of boredom that presents no challenge to his sharp mentality.

The Cocker Spaniel is an obedience trial dog par excellence, and few breeds have better records in the obedience trials. In training, either for the field or for obedience, hard-headedness is always a problem to the trainer, who has to force the training down the dog's throat in spite of his disinterest or unwillingness. Fortunately that characteristic is entirely foreign to the Cocker's nature. He takes to training with

PHOTO BY ISABELLE FRANCAIS.

It's a dog's life! This sleepy Cocker seems to have had a long day.

PHOTO BY VINCE SERBIN.

The merry, adaptable Cocker Spaniel has as much fun playing with children as he does tramping in the woods following the scent of game.

vim, enjoying every minute of it with his stub of a tail beating a mile a minute. Again, he'll break his neck to please his master and is never happier than when he can be with him with a job to do.

HOUSING FOR YOUR COCKER

No special housing is necessary for the Cocker Spaniel. He can live in a heated apartment or in an unheated outside kennel in sub-zero weather. But he must be acclimated gradually to one or the other with no sudden shifts. If a Cocker is kept out-of-doors in northern areas in the winter, he must have a small (large enough to stand up, lie down, and turn around, but no larger) kennel with several thicknesses of burlap sacking tacked across the top of the door, so that it will fall back into place after the dog has entered. There should be a good quantity of straw into which the dog can burrow. Also, he must have plenty of room to run and exercise. A dog living outside in the winter must not be tied up; he must be able to run to keep the blood circulating.

PHOTO BY ISABELLE FRANCAIS.

Laura Heidrich poses with her two beautiful buff Cocker Spaniels.

STANDARD FOR THE BREED

A breed standard is the criterion by which the appearance (and to a certain extent, the temperament as well) of any given dog is made subject to objective measurement. Basically, the standard for any breed is a definition of the perfect dog, to which all specimens of the breed are compared. Breed standards are always subject to change through review by the national breed club for each dog, so it is always wise to keep up with developments in a breed by checking the publications of your national kennel club.

Both the American Kennel Club and The Kennel Club (Great Britain) have approved standards for the Cocker Spaniel, although it should be noted that in England the breed is known as the American Cocker Spaniel. The requirements as given in both standards are essentially the same, except that the British version permits a small amount of white on the chest and throat of a solid-colored dog, and is somewhat more liberal concerning maximum height by simply penalizing rather than disqualifying excessive height. It is, of course, recommended that the owner of a Cocker become thoroughly familiar with the official standard of the national club under which the dog is registered or will be shown.

THE AMERICAN KENNEL CLUB STANDARD

General Appearance: The Cocker Spaniel is the smallest member of the Sporting Group. He has a sturdy, compact body and a cleanly chiseled and refined head, with the overall dog in complete balance and of ideal size. He stands well up at the shoulder on straight forelegs with a topline sloping slightly toward strong, muscular quarters. He is a dog capable of considerable speed, combined with great endurance. Above all he must be free and merry, sound, well balanced throughout, and in action show a keen inclination to work; equable in temperament with no suggestion of timidity.

Head: To attain a well-proportioned head, which must be in balance with the rest of the

PHOTO BY ISABELLE FRANCAIS.

This parti-colored Cocker shows the cleanly chiseled and refined head that is called for in the standard. Owner, David Eversmann.

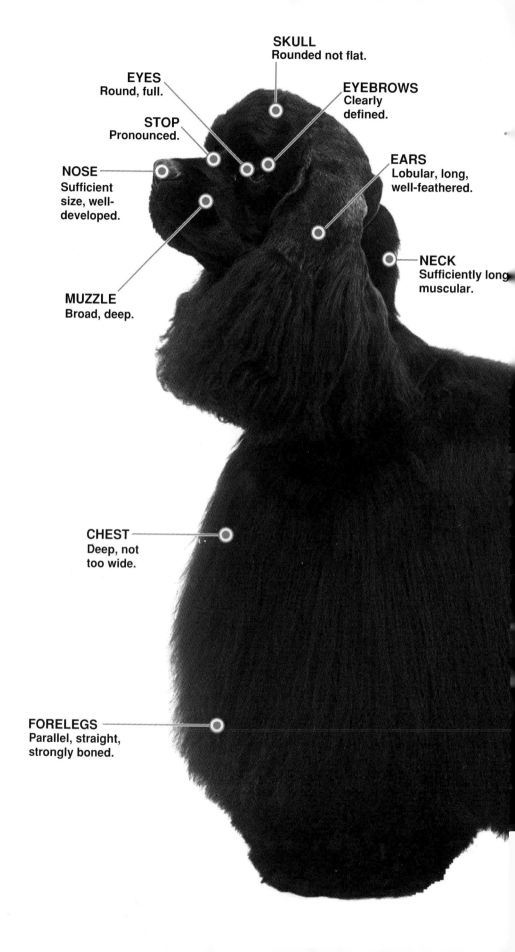

SKULL
Rounded not flat.

EYES
Round, full.

EYEBROWS
Clearly
defined.

STOP
Pronounced.

EARS
Lobular, long,
well-feathered.

NOSE
Sufficient
size, well-
developed.

NECK
Sufficiently long
muscular.

MUZZLE
Broad, deep.

CHEST
Deep, not
too wide.

FORELEGS
Parallel, straight,
strongly boned.

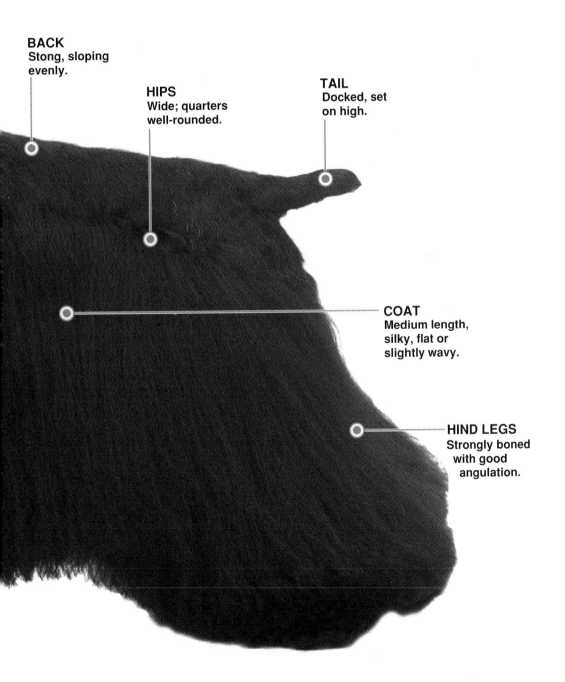

1994 Westminster Best of Breed winner Ch. Westglen Blak-Gammon owned by Corliss Westerman and Tracy Lynn Carroll.

BACK
Stong, sloping
evenly.

HIPS
Wide; quarters
well-rounded.

TAIL
Docked, set
on high.

COAT
Medium length,
silky, flat or
slightly wavy.

HIND LEGS
Strongly boned
with good
angulation.

This is Ch. LGE's Patek Philippe, the 1994 Westminster Best of Breed winner, ASCOB variety. Owner, Linda Gruskin.

sporting dog. It is black in color in the blacks and black and tans. In other colors it may be brown, liver or black, the darker the better. The color of the nose harmonizes with the color of the eye rim. *Eyes*—Eyeballs are round and full and look directly forward. The shape of the eye rims gives a slightly almond-shaped appearance; the eye is not weak or goggled. The color of the iris is dark brown and in general the darker the better. The expression is intelligent, alert, soft and appealing. *Ears*—Lobular, long, of fine leather, well feathered, and placed no higher than a line to the lower part of the eye.

Neck and Shoulders: The neck is sufficiently long to allow the nose to reach the ground easily, muscular and free from

Head study of Ch. Kane Venture Heaven Gait, the 1994 Westminster Best of Breed winner, parti-color variety. Owners, C. Paul, Sandy Bailey, and Diana Kane.

dog, it embodies the following: *Skull*—Rounded but not exaggerated with no tendency toward flatness; the eyebrows are clearly defined with a pronounced stop. The bony structure beneath the eyes is well chiseled with no prominence in the cheeks. *Muzzle*—Broad and deep, with square, even jaws. The upper lip is full and of sufficient depth to cover the lower jaw. To be in correct balance, the distance from the stop to the tip of the nose is one half the distance from the stop up over the crown to the base of the skull. *Teeth*—Strong and sound, not too small, and meet in a scissors bite. *Nose*—Of sufficient size to balance the muzzle and foreface, with well-developed nostrils typical of a

Notice this Cocker's silky, wavy coat and feathered chest and legs as called for in the standard. Owned by Joseph J. Nowak.

The Cocker Spaniel's neck should rise strongly from the shoulders and be long enough to allow the nose to reach the ground easily. Owner, Lee Perron.

pendulous "throatiness." It rises strongly from the shoulders and arches slightly as it tapers to join the head. The shoulders are well laid back forming an angle with the upper arm of approximately 90 degrees which permits the dog to move his forelegs in an easy manner with considerable forward reach. Shoulders are cleancut and sloping without protrusion and so set that the upper points of the withers are at an angle which permits a wide spring of rib.

Body: The body is short, compact and firmly knit together, giving an impression of strength. The distance from the highest point of the shoulder blades to the ground is fifteen percent or approximately two inches more than the length from this point to the set-on of the tail. Back is strong and sloping evenly and slightly downward from the shoulders to the set-on of the docked tail. Hips are wide and quarters well rounded and muscular. The chest is deep, its lowest point no higher than the elbows, its front sufficiently wide for adequate heart and lung space, yet not so wide as to interfere with the straight forward movement of the forelegs. Ribs are deep and well sprung. The Cocker Spaniel never appears long and low. *Tail*—The docked tail is set on and carried on a line with the topline of the back, or slightly higher; never straight up like a terrier and never so low as to indicate timidity. When the dog is in motion the tail action is merry. *Legs*—Forelegs are parallel, straight, strongly boned and muscular and set close to the

The Cocker's feet need to be compact, large, round and firm—these attributes make for tireless, efficient hunting. Owner, April Stich.

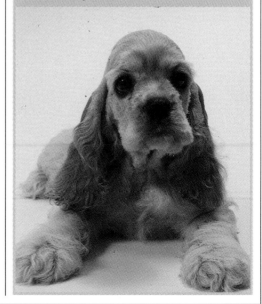

body well under the scapulae. When viewed from the side with the forelegs vertical, the elbow is directly below the highest point of the shoulder blade. The pasterns are short and strong. The hind legs are strongly boned and muscled with good angulation at the stifle and powerful, clearly defined thighs. The stifle joint is strong and there is no slippage of it in motion or when standing. The hocks are strong, well let down, and when viewed from behind, the hind legs are parallel when in motion and at rest. *Feet*—Compact, large, round and firm with horny pads; they turn neither in nor out. Dewclaws on hind legs and forelegs may be removed.

Coat: On the head, short and fine; on the body, medium length, with enough undercoating to give protection. The ears, chest, abdomen and legs are well feathered, but not so excessively as to hide the Cocker Spaniel's true lines and movement or affect his appearance and function as a sporting dog. The *texture* is most important. The coat is silky, flat or slightly wavy, and of a texture which permits

PHOTO BY ISABELLE FRANCAIS.

Cocker Spaniels come in three varieties: black, any solid color other than black (ASCOB), and parti-colored. This Cocker is considered parti-colored, which is a coat of white plus one or more colors. Owner, Margaret Hawvermale.

easy care. Excessive or curly or cottony textured coat is to be penalized.

Color and Markings: *Black Variety*—Solid color black, to include black with tan points. The black should be jet; shadings of brown or liver in the sheen of the coat is not desirable. A small amount of white on the chest and/or throat is allowed, white in any other location shall disqualify. *Any Solid Color Other Than Black*— Any solid color other than black and any such color with tan points. The color shall be of a uniform shade, but lighter coloring of the feather is permissible. A small amount of white on the chest and/or throat is allowed, white in any other location shall disqualify. *Parti-Color Variety*—Two or more definite, well-broken colors, one of which must be white, including those with tan points; it is preferable that the tan markings be located in the same pattern as for the tan points in the Black and ASCOB varieties. Roans are classified as parti-colors, and may be of any of the usual roaning patterns. Primary color which is ninety percent or more shall disqualify. *Tan Points*—The color of the tan may be from the lightest cream to the darkest red color and should be restricted to ten percent or less of the color of the specimen, tan markings in excess of that amount shall disqualify.

In the case of tan points in the Black or ASCOB variety, the markings shall be located as follows:

(1) A clear tan spot over each eye

(2) On the sides of the muzzle and on the cheeks

(3) On the undersides of the ears

(4) On all feet and/or legs

The ideal height of the Cocker is 15 inches for dogs and 14 inches for bitches. Owner, Xiomara Larson.

The Cocker Spaniel's eyes are round, full, and dark brown. Expression is intelligent, alert, soft, and appealing. This Cocker exhibits all of those qualities. Owner, Ellen O'Connor.

(5) Under the tail

(6) On the chest (optional, presence or absence not penalized). Tan markings which are not readily visible or which amount only to traces, shall be penalized. Tan on the muzzle which extends upward, over and joins shall also be penalized. The absence of tan markings in the Black or ASCOB variety in each of the specified locations in an otherwise tan-pointed dog shall disqualify.

Movement: The Cocker Spaniel, though the smallest of the sporting dogs, possesses a typical sporting dog gait. Prerequisite to good movement is balance between the front and rear assemblies. He drives with his strong, powerful rear quarters and is properly constructed in the

PHOTO BY ISABELLE FRANCAIS.

The Cocker's skull is rounded, and the muzzle is broad and deep with square, even jaws.

shoulders and forelegs so that he can reach forward without constriction in a full stride to counterbalance the driving force from the rear. Above all, his gait is coordinated, smooth and effortless. The dog must cover ground with his action and excessive animation should never be mistaken for proper gait.

Height: The ideal height at the withers for an adult dog is 15 inches and for an adult bitch 14 inches. Height may vary one-half inch above or below this ideal. A dog whose height exceeds 15½ inches or a bitch whose height exceeds 14½ inches shall be disqualified. An adult dog whose height is less than 14½ inches or an adult bitch whose height is less than 13½ inches shall be penalized. *Note:* Height is determined by a line perpendicular to the ground from the top of the shoulder blades, the dog standing naturally with its forelegs and the lower hind legs parallel to the line of measurement.

DISQUALIFICATIONS
COLOR AND MARKINGS

Blacks—White markings except on chest and throat.

Any Solid Color Other Than Black Variety—White markings except on chest and throat.

Tan Points—(1) Tan markings excess of ten percent; (2)Absence of tan markings in black or ASCOB variety in any of the specified locations in an otherwise tan pointed dog.'

Parti-Color Variety—Ninety percent or more of primary color.

HEIGHT—Males over 15½ inches; females over 14½ inches.

PHOTO BY ISABELLE FRANCAIS.

The Cocker Spaniel's ears are long, lobular, well feathered, and of fine leather. Owner, Linda Schnabel.

Keeping your Cocker's coat as neat and squeaky clean as this takes a little time but is well worth the effort.

COCKER SPANIEL GROOMING

BATHING

Use tepid water, an ordinary hose spray that fastens to the bathtub faucet, and only those soaps specifically designed for use in bathing dogs. Soak the dog thoroughly and then shampoo in the soap, massaging vigorously. (Be careful not to get water into the ear canal.) Then rinse until the water comes off the dog perfectly clear and the coat is "squeaky clean." Dry well with two turkish towels. Keep the dog out of drafts until completely dry. That's all there is to bathing.

Grooming, on the other hand, is very important and should be a daily chore. The thought to keep in mind is that the more often the coat is groomed, the easier grooming becomes. Once you let dead hair become matted, you have a job on your hands.

PHOTO BY ISABELLE FRANCAIS.

Grooming should begin during puppyhood so that your Cocker Spaniel is comfortable with the procedure.

Brushing your Cocker Spaniel for a few minutes every day will simplify grooming sessions and keep the coat looking clean and healthy.

PHOTO BY ISABELLE FRANCAIS.

GROOMING TOOLS

Your tools are a stiff, steel-toothed comb about 7 inches long, a stiff-bristled brush, and, if you like, a slicker brush, which is a flat metal brush with many fine steel bristles and a handle. It resembles a horse's curry comb and is used the same way. It is all right for a quick job, but not as thorough as the comb and brush. Give the coat a good going-over

TRIMMING YOUR COCKER SPANIEL

Now let's talk about trimming. As a minimum, if you'll trim the hair around the feet and between the pads, the dog will bring the least dirt into the house. That's easy to do. The only other really necessary attention is the ear canals, and it is essential that they be cleaned out as needed. Use ordinary cotton applicators and

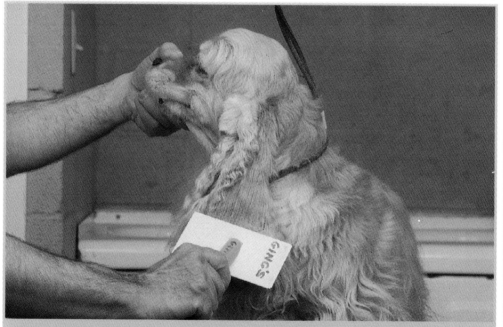

Use a slicker brush on a daily basis to comb out all dead hair. If you have the time for a more thorough job, be sure to also use a comb and brush.

daily, being sure to comb out all dead hair, and your Cocker will always maintain a good appearance and your friends will ask how you keep such a good coat on your dog. Let me emphasize the grooming chore is a matter of ten or fifteen minutes if done daily; but it's a long job as a once-a-month proposition.

alcohol and swab the canals being careful not to dig too deeply. Then dry with fresh applicators and cotton swabs around the ear. If, however, you want to maintain the dog in a barbered trim you will need some tools—and experience. A double-edged instrument, using certain safety razor blades (used with a shaving motion along the

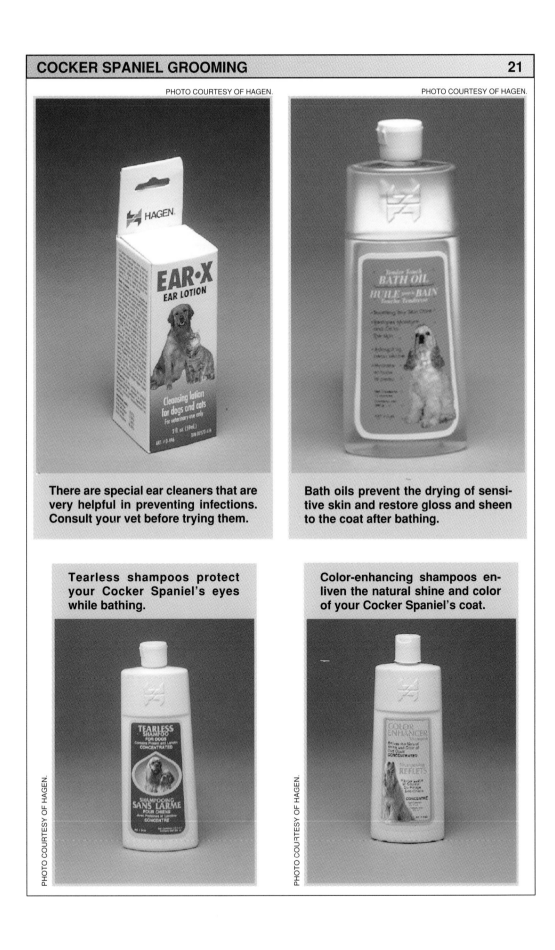

There are special ear cleaners that are very helpful in preventing infections. Consult your vet before trying them.

Bath oils prevent the drying of sensitive skin and restore gloss and sheen to the coat after bathing.

Tearless shampoos protect your Cocker Spaniel's eyes while bathing.

Color-enhancing shampoos enliven the natural shine and color of your Cocker Spaniel's coat.

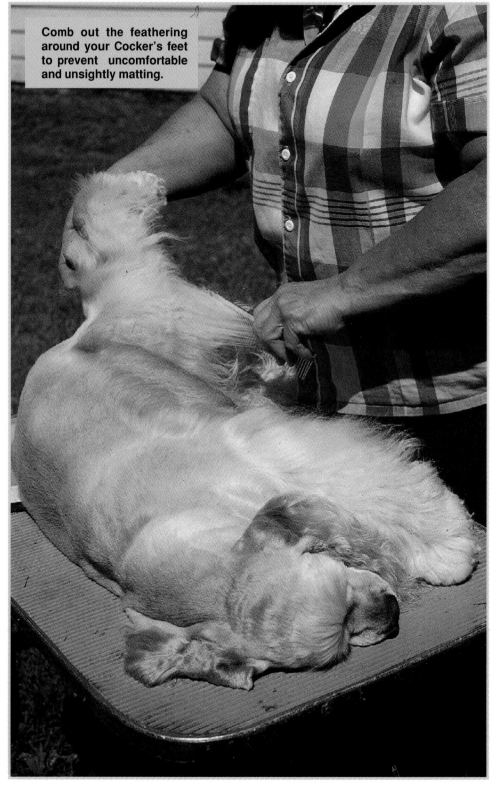

PHOTO COURTESY OF HAGEN.

Comb out the feathering around your Cocker's feet to prevent uncomfortable and unsightly matting.

lay of the hair), plus a comb, are really the only instruments you need, though you can go on to thinning scissors, clippers, etc.

Starting with the dog's muzzle, take the hair down along both sides, along his underjaw and neck, and along the cheeks and over the skull. Watch your trimming and accentuate the length.

From the base of the skull trim the neck, top, and sides, so that it seems to slide into trim, neat shoulders. In front, trim rather closely to a point where the neck disappears into the chest. In general, follow the same procedure over the body and hind legs, removing fuzziness but not chopping the coat. Clean out the

PHOTO COURTESY OF WAHL CLIPPER.

The Cocker Spaniel coat can be a high-maintenance job. Choose the best grooming tools from your local pet shop.

graduate the short with the longer hair so that no sharp line of demarcation is evident. Start where the ear joins the skull and trim rather closely down along the outer surface for about two inches. Turn the ear up and trim out the tuft of hair under the ear; the idea is to have the ear lie close to the head and to hair around and under the tail and the "feather" at the end of the tail. It is assumed that you have already trimmed around the paws.

Trimming does take practice, but it certainly is not beyond average dexterity, and a well-trimmed Cocker is a beauty to behold.

Grooming should be a joy, not a chore, as it is time you can spend to bond with your Cocker Spaniel.

THE SPORTING COCKER

In addition to being a merry little house dog that is perfect for cuddling warmth, the Cocker Spaniel is a dog full of exciting energy. Considering the vibrance and athleticism contained in this breed, it is no wonder that the Cocker not only excels as a family pet and conformation dog, but also in several other activities. Versatility is a word that well describes the Cocker Spaniel, for this dog can be utilized in any of a number of competitions and tasks.

OBEDIENCE

When talking about the Cocker Spaniel in competition, you must begin with the obedience ring, where they have performed well since the 1940s. The second most popular event in the dog sport, obedience trials consider a dog's skill, training, and interaction with man. These trials, held all over the world by national organizations such as the AKC as well as local clubs, involve all types of dogs and provide education and entertainment for both the dogs involved and the spectators. What the dog looks like has nothing to do with this kind of competition—only his ability to perform the various tasks. A complete series of exercises and activities are

PHOTO BY ISABELLE FRANCAIS.

Owing to its origins as a gun dog, the Cocker Spaniel is an athletic canine that enjoys outdoor activities.

included, and a judge appoints a score according to how well each assignment was executed. The versatile Cocker Spaniel has proved itself in all aspects of obedience, which includes not only the ability to follow basic commands but also more advanced skills. To explain, there are three levels of obedience competition: Novice, Open, and Utility, each an exceeding level of difficulty. For example, the Novice level consists of fundamental behavior exercises such as heel on leash, stand for examination, heel free, recall, long sit, and long down. The next level focuses on more demanding feats of obedience and agility, including retrieving, retrieving over high jump, and the broad jump. The most advanced level (Utility) involves five activities: signal exercise, scent discrimination, directed retrieve, directed jumping, and group examination.

alone as an exercise. While most of the tasks in obedience are comprised of skills that can be taught, tracking is more of an inherent talent that must be developed. As stated in the *AKC Guidelines for Obedience Judges,* *"Tracking is a sport in the truest sense. The animal works for the sheer love of scenting. No dog can*

The dog sport has always been first and foremost conformation shows—obedience and tracking became popular in the 1940's.

As you can see, getting involved in obedience competition will truly test the merits of your Cocker Spaniel and also be a fun time for both you and your pet.

TRACKING

Another activity for you and your Cocker is tracking. Tracking is actually related to the aforementioned obedience competition, but because of its nature and following it stands

be forced to track." Because Cocker Spaniels have excellent scenting abilities and take great pleasure in following a trail, they are naturals for tracking.

Since very few Cocker Spaniels learn how to use their nose until they are about six months of age, tracking training should begin then. Even if you're not ready to enter a tracking competition, you can still have a lot of fun making tracks for your Cocker to follow;

all it takes is open area and a little creativity. Try to find a large grassy field or woodlands to lay your track. Equipment needed includes a comfortable nylon harness, a 10-40-foot lead, liver treats (or any other treat your Cocker enjoys), about six dowels or similar items to use as markers, and a few different types from your dog. Stake a marker into the ground and place an item (wallet, etc.) next to it with a treat underneath. Next, walk back to your Cocker in a straight line along your original path and start tracking. Your Cocker should be able to follow the smell of the treat that came off of your feet. When your Cocker finally sniffs

PHOTO BY ROBERT SMITH.

Tracking is a competition in which the Cocker performs very well. Try to find a large grassy field or similar open field for laying a practice track.

of personal articles, such as leather and cloth gloves, socks, a belt, shoes, a wallet, eyeglass case, etc. Once you find a good track, try to go to it on a dry comfortable day, and without spectators or any other distractions. When you get there, find a place to tie your Cocker up while you set out to lay the track. Begin by rubbing the treat onto your the soles of your shoes, and slowly walk out about 30 yards out the article and treat, praise him generously. During this process, be sure to keep yourself quiet until your dog finds the item as giving commands or praise while tracking will likely confuse the dog, at least in the beginning stages of training. If your Cocker is successful in sniffing out his first 30-yard track, then try to lay one or two more that are a few yards longer, using the same method. Three easy tracks are

A high-quality leash is essential when training your Cocker Spaniel outdoors. Visit your local pet shop to choose one that best suits your needs.

enough for the first day.

Should you and your Cocker find these beginning lessons enjoyable, you may want to learn more about tracking, laying tracks, and maybe even getting involved in tracking competition. If so, there are a number of books available on the subject of tracking, as well as many organizations devoted to tracking specifically. Getting in touch with one of these tracking organizations, as well as your local Cocker Spaniel club, are the first steps in serious tracking. Tracking is fun, great exercise,

and lets your Cocker be the sporting dog it was meant to be. Not only that, but you'll never again have to worry about finding a lost item.

AGILITY

A more vigorous activity your Cocker Spaniel can engage in is agility. Agility is based on stadium jumping competitions that horses engage in. Dogs run through a complex obstacle course and are scored according to how quickly and accurately they can complete the course. The winner is the dog that completes the course in the fastest time with the fewest faults. Faults can include anything from taking the obstacles in the wrong order to refusing to attempt an obstacle.

The obstacles are built in different sizes according to the size of the dog. For example, your diminutive Cocker Spaniel would run the same course as a much larger Labrador Retriever, except

Looks like this Cocker has sniffed out his game and is about to flush!

PHOTO BY KAREN TAYLOR.

The athleticism of the Cocker Spaniel is truly apparent in agility competition. Here a Cocker is leaping over the bar jump.

the obstacles would be placed at different heights and lengths. Objects on the agility course include an A-frame, hoop, rigid and collapsible tunnels, scaling wall, seesaw, table or pause box (where the dog must stand on top for five seconds), and jumps. Although an agility course obviously takes much more equipment and room than other activities, an industrious owner with a large backyard can build his own obstacles from simple items like wooden boards, two-by-fours, and old tires. It may seem like a lot of work, but the pleasure you'll get from watching your Cocker conquer his new course will be worth the effort. Of course, as with any vigorous exercise, be sure your Cocker Spaniel is physically mature and in good shape before you begin any serious training.

HUNTING DOG

For those of you interested in the practical aspects of the Cocker Spaniel, look no further than the original use of the breed: as a hunting dog. The profusely merry temperament and cutesy-cuddliness of the breed has transformed the Cocker Spaniel into a popular house pet and veritable show dog. However, we must not overlook this breed's suitability as a bonafide gundog.

At about eight weeks of age, the Cocker Spaniel puppy is already a natural retriever, and will happily

The Cocker Spaniel is a natural retriever and will happily chase after anything from a ball to a bird.

PHOTO BY ROBERT SMITH.

chase after a ball, bone, or other toy. If eventually you want to bring your Cocker on hunting trips, now is the time to encourage fetching bird-like items, such as a canvas dummy with bird wings taped to it. Make sure the dummy is small enough for your puppy to grab and hold in his mouth. To get really authentic, you can even introduce live birds; allow your Cocker pup to chase homing pigeons. *No shooting should be done at this time!* Do make sure that you properly train your Cocker to recall on command before you allow him to run about freely. After a few retrieving sessions, you may want to begin water

retrieval—just make sure the water isn't too cold. A young Cocker pup will take to swimming as long it has been made familiar to water. To ensure this, go into the water with your dog in the beginning, until your Cocker seems to be comfortable and fearless in the water. Soon he will begin swimming, at which point you may begin tossing sticks, bird dummies, or other objects into the water for your Cocker to retrieve. If all is going well at this point and you'd really like to get your Cocker involved in your hunting trips, then it would be a good idea to read a few books on the subject of training gundogs and to get involved in a sporting/hunting club in your area. The most important thing to keep in mind, if you intend to hunt with your Cocker Spaniel, is that obedience

A natural hunting dog, the Cocker Spaniel can also be very effective in several other areas due to his high intelligence, athleticism, and willingness to please.

PHOTO BY ISABELLE FRANCAIS.

Remember that obedience is the foundation of all training, regardless of which activity your Cocker participates in.

training is the foundation. No matter how brilliant your Cocker is at flushing game, the skill is useless if you cannot control him.

Remember that your Cocker Spaniel is not limited to the activities that involve hunting and competitions. On the contrary, the Cocker Spaniel is so bright, agile, and willing to please, he can be taught most any task to help out around the home. Simple jobs such as bringing in the newspaper, putting away your slippers, and finding the remote control (what a practical idea!) are all ably and competently handled by the Cocker Spaniel. Keep in mind that the Cocker Spaniel is naturally an outdoor dog, and was originally bred to be a viable companion to the hunter, so his talents of practicality are virtually limitless.

YOUR COCKER'S HEALTH

We know our pets, their moods and habits, and therefore we can recognize when our Cocker is experiencing an off-day. Signs of sickness can be very obvious or very subtle. As any mother can attest, diagnosing and treating an ailment requires common sense, knowing when to seek home remedies and when to visit your veterinarian.

Your veterinarian, we know, is your Cocker's best friend, next to you. It will pay to be choosy about your veterinarian. Talk to dog-owning friends whom you respect. Visit more than one vet before you make a lifelong choice. Trust your instincts. Find a knowledgeable, compassionate vet who knows Cocker Spaniels and likes them.

Given the Cocker's long ears, big beautiful eyes, abundant coat, and certain other possible inherited disorders, an owner must pay special attention to the following:

Always check your Cocker's ears, as regular cleaning and conscientious observation is the key to preventing ear problems. Because the Cocker's ears are so long and heavily feathered, they are more prone to irritation and infection than most other breeds. Routine bathing of the ears with equal parts hydrogen peroxide and rubbing alcohol twice a week proves very effective. Pet shops sell ear cleansers that work nicely.

PHOTO BY ISABELLE FRANCAIS.

The Cocker Spaniel's long ears have a tendency to accumulate oils and dirt and are prone to infection. Regular inspection will prevent any unwanted afflictions.

Cocker's eyes are prone to injury as well as certain predisposed faults, such as cherry eyes (hypertrophy of nicitans glands) which affect puppies of short-nosed breeds. If the signs of cherry eye are caught, steroid ointment prevent further irritation so as to avoid surgery.

Cockers are also prone to closed tear ducts, which may or may not require veterinary care. When the duct closes, the eyes will tear. While tearing is not always a sign of closed ducts, it's still a good idea to have your vet take a look.

Conjunctivitis, the irritation of the pink tissue that lines the eyes from foreign matter or bacteria, is not an uncommon problem for Cockers. Keep your Cocker's eyes free of straggly hairs by trimming around them, and wash them frequently with warm water.

When grooming your Cocker, check the skin for lesions, tumors, or other growths. A chronic bacterial problem known as staph dermatitis is reported in Cockers and is treatable. Frequent baths are helpful to the Cocker to reduce irritation, itching or erythema—as well as management of doggy odor. Always check for fleas and ticks, especially after the dog has been outside. The Cocker's coat is thick and provides a wonderful breeding ground for unwanted parasites. Remember, the smallest flea or tick can lead to a variety of internal parasitic problems, such as heartworm or Lyme disease. Also check the feet for interdigital cysts, which are fairly common in Cocker Spaniels.

Anal sacs, sometimes called anal glands, are located in the musculature of the anal ring, one on either side. Each empties into the rectum via a small duct. Occasionally their secretion becomes thickened and accumulates so you can readily feel these structures from the outside. If your Cocker is scooting across the floor dragging his rear quarters, or licking his rear, his anal sacs may need to be expressed. Placing pressure in and up towards the anus, while holding the tail, is the general routine. Anal sac secretions are characteristically foul-smelling, and you could get squirted if not careful. Veterinarians can take care of this during regular visits and demonstrate the cleanest method.

Many Cockers are predisposed to certain congenital and inherited abnormalities, such as hip dysplasia, a blatantly common problem in purebred dogs with few exceptions. Von Willebrand's disease is a bleeding disorder which can be managed. The eyes are prone to cataracts, glaucoma, and entropion. Other problems, such as facial paralysis, epilepsy and hypothyroidism, affect some lines more commonly than others. Ask the breeder for records of any of these problems before acquiring a puppy.

PHOTO COURTESY OF HAGEN.

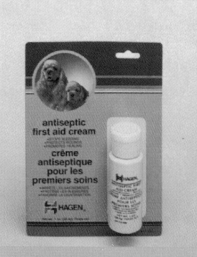

You should always have first-aid supplies handy, especially for the active Cocker Spaniel. Your local pet shop carries a full line of emergency supplies.

For the continued health of your Cocker Spaniel, owners must attend to vaccinations regularly. Your veterinarian can recommend a vaccination schedule appropriate for your dog taking into consideration the factors of climate and geography. The basic vaccinations to protect your Cocker are: parvovirus, distemper, hepatitis, leptospirosis, adenovirus, parainfluenza, coronavirus, bordetella, tracheo-bronchitis (kennel cough), Lyme disease and rabies.

Parvovirus is a highly contagious, dog-specific disease, first recognized in 1978. Targeting the small intestine, parvo affects the stomach and diarrhea and vomiting (with blood) are clinical signs. Although the dog can pass the infection to other dogs within three days of infection, the initial signs, which include lethargy and depression, don't display themselves until four to seven days. When affecting puppies under four weeks of age, the heart muscle is frequently attacked. When the heart is affected, the puppies exhibit

PHOTO BY PAULETTE BRAUN.

Always brush out and inspect your Cocker's coat after any time spent in woodlands or areas of heavy foliage. These kinds of regions are the breeding grounds of ticks and mites.

difficulty in breathing and experience crying and foaming at the nose and mouth.

Distemper, related to human measles, is an airborne virus that spreads in the blood and ultimately in the nervous system and epithelial tissues. Young dogs or dogs with weak immune systems can develop encephalomyelitis (brain disease) from the distemper infection. Such dogs experience seizures, general weakness and rigidity, as well as "hardpad." Since distemper is largely incurable, prevention through vaccination is vitally important. Puppies should be vaccinated at six to eight weeks of age, with boosters at ten to 12 weeks. Older puppies (16 weeks and older) who are unvaccinated should receive no fewer than two vaccinations at three to four week intervals.

Hepatitis mainly affects the liver and is caused by canine adenovirus type I. Highly infectious, hepatitis often affects dogs nine to 12 months of age. Initially the virus localizes in the dog's tonsils and then disperses to the liver, kidney and eyes. Generally speaking the dog's immune system is capable of combating this virus. Canine infectious hepatitis affects dogs whose systems cannot fight off the adenovirus. Affected dogs have fever, abdominal pains, bruising on mucous membranes and gums, and experience coma and convulsions. Prevention of hepatitis exists only through vaccination at eight to ten weeks of age and then boosters three or four weeks later, then annually.

Leptospirosis is a bacterium-related disease, often spread by rodents. The organisms that spread leptospirosis enter through the mucous membrane and spread to the internal organs via the bloodstream. It can be passed through the dog's urine. Leptospirosis does not affect young dogs as consistently as the other viruses; it is reportedly regional in distribution and somewhat dependent on the immunostatus of the dog. Fever, inappetence, vomiting, dehydration, hemorrhage, kidney and eye disease can result in moderate cases.

Coronavirus is a type of digestive upset that is similar to, but much milder than, parvovirus infection. Once acquired by the affected dog, the virus spreads throughout the small intestine within four days. Symptoms include poor appetite, lethargy, vomiting, diarrhea, and dehydration. The digestive upset can persist or be intermittent for three to four weeks, after which most dogs will recover completely within seven to ten days. The main fear with this particular virus is the possibility of dehydration, which can be fatal. In this case, fluids are essential to replace the electrolytes lost. There is a vaccine available for this virus, and it is typically given at six, nine, and 12 weeks of age. Other than administering the vaccine, the best way to avoid this potentially devastating disease is to keep the dog's environment clean. Because the virus is shed in the feces, dogs that are prone to coprophagia (eating feces) must be monitored in areas that are frequented by strange dogs, and daily cleaning of your Cocker's premises with a bleach and water solution is effective in deactivating coronavirus. Also, feeding your dog inside and keeping food safe from contamination by flies, roaches, and other insects will aid in decreasing the spread of the virus.

Parainfluenza is a virus that infects the respiratory system and combines with any of several other viruses to cause canine or kennel cough. Parainfluenza and other viruses spread rapidly, and the Cocker is particularly susceptible. These types of viruses are very often contracted in large housing kennels where dogs are in close contact with each other, and therefore the disease is often referred to as "kennel cough." This disease can also be transmitted to and from cats.

Bordetella, called canine cough, causes a persistent hacking cough in dogs and is very contagious. Bordetella involves a virus and a bacteria: parainfluenza is the most common virus implicated; *Bordetella bronchiseptica*, the bacterium. Bronchitis and pneumonia result in less than 20 percent of the cases, and most dogs recover from the condition within a week to four weeks. Non-prescription medicines can help relieve the hacking cough, though nothing can cure the condition before it's run its course. Vaccination cannot guarantee protection from canine cough, but it does ward off the most common virus that is responsible for the condition.

Lyme disease (also called borreliosis), although known for decades, was only first diagnosed in dogs in 1984. Lyme disease can affect cats, cattle, and horses, but especially people. In the US, the disease is transmitted by two ticks carrying the *Borrelia burgdorferi* organism: the deer

Combing your Cocker on a daily basis with a high-quality brush or comb will help thwart parasitic invasion and skin diseases.

Applying a good flea and tick shampoo will help prevent infestation of your Cocker's coat.

tick (*Ixodes scapularis*) and the western black-legged tick (*Ixodes pacificus*), the latter primarily affects reptiles. In Europe, *Ixodes ricinus* is responsible for spreading Lyme. The disease causes lameness, fever, joint swelling, inappetence, and lethargy. Removal of ticks from the dog's coat can help reduce the chances of Lyme, though not as much as avoiding heavily wooded areas where the dog is most likely to contract ticks. A vaccination is available, though it has not been proven to protect dogs from all strains of the organism that causes the disease.

Rabies is passed to dogs and people through wildlife: in North America, principally through the skunk, fox and raccoon; the bat is not the culprit it was once thought to be. Likewise, the common image of the rabid dog foaming at the mouth with every hair on end is unlikely the truest scenario. A rabid dog exhibits difficulty eating, salivates much and has spells of paralysis and awkwardness. Before a dog reaches this final state, it may experience anxiety, personality changes, irritability and more aggressiveness than is usual. Vaccinations are strongly recommended as affected dogs are too dangerous to manage and are commonly euthanized. Puppies are generally vaccinated at 12 weeks of age, and then annually. Although rabies is on the decline in the world community, tens of thousands of humans die each year from rabies-related incidents.

PHOTO BY PAULETTE BRAUN.

Be sure to choose a reputable veterinarian and keep up on vaccination schedules to ensure the health of your Cocker Spaniel.

FEEDING

Now let's talk about feeding your Cocker Spaniel, a subject so simple that it's amazing there is so much nonsense and misunderstanding about it. Is it expensive to feed a Cocker Spaniel? No, it is not! You can feed your Cocker Spaniel economically and keep him in perfect shape the year round, or you can feed him expensively. He'll thrive either way, and let's see why this is true.

First of all, remember a Cocker Spaniel is a dog. Dogs do not have a high degree of selectivity in their food, and unless you spoil them with great variety (and possibly turn them into poor, "picky" eaters) they will eat almost anything that they become accustomed to. Many dogs flatly refuse to eat nice, fresh beef. They pick around it and eat everything else. But meat—bah! Why? They aren't accustomed to it! They'd eat rabbit fast enough, but they refuse beef because they aren't used to it.

PHOTO BY ISABELLE FRANCAIS.

Feeding your Cocker Spaniel should not be a major dilemma. Choose a quality brand of dry dog food and avoid giving human treats, unless you'd like a picky pet.

VARIETY NOT NECESSARY

A good general rule of thumb is forget all human preferences and don't give a thought to variety. Choose the right diet for your Cocker Spaniel and feed it to him day after day, year after year, winter and summer. But what is the right diet?

Hundreds of thousands of dollars have been spent in canine nutrition research. The results are pretty conclusive, so you needn't go into a lot of experimenting with trials of this and that every other week. Research has proven just what your dog needs to eat and to keep healthy.

DOG FOOD

There are almost as many right diets as there are dog experts, but the basic diet most often recommended is one that consists of a dry food, either meal or kibble form. There are several of excellent quality, manufactured by reliable companies, research tested, and nationally advertised. They are inexpensive, highly satisfactory, and easily available in stores everywhere in containers of five to 50 pounds. Larger amounts cost less per pound, usually.

If you have a choice of brands, it is usually safer to choose the better known one; but even so, carefully read the analysis on the package. Do not choose any food in which the protein level is less than 25 percent, and be sure that this protein comes from both animal and vegetable sources. The good dog foods have meat meal, fish meal, liver, and such, plus protein from alfalfa and soy beans, as well as some dried-milk product. Note the vitamin content carefully. See that they are all there in good proportions; and be especially certain that the food contains properly high levels of vitamins A and D, two of the most perishable and important ones.

Note the B-complex level, but don't worry about carbohydrate and mineral levels. These substances are plentiful and cheap and not likely to be lacking in a good brand.

The advice given for how to choose a dry food also applies to moist or canned types of dog foods, if you decide to feed one of these.

Having chosen a really good food, feed it to your Cocker Spaniel as the manufacturer directs. And once you've started, stick to it. Never change if you can possibly help it. A switch from one meal or kibble-type food can usually be made without too much upset; however, a change

PHOTO BY ISABELLE FRANCAIS.

Unlike the strictly carnivorous cat, the dog is generally an omnivorous creature, and most will happily eat dog foods that contain items such as alfalfa and soybeans.

Your Cocker Spaniel puppy will require slight alterations in diet as he grows. However, once he develops into a full-grown adult, there should be very little change or variety in his victuals.

will almost invariably give you (and your Cocker Spaniel) some trouble.

WHEN SUPPLEMENTS ARE NEEDED

Now what about supplements of various kinds, mineral and vitamin, or the various oils? They are all okay to add to your Cocker Spaniel's food. However, if you are feeding your Cocker Spaniel a correct diet, and this is easy to do, no supplements are necessary unless your Cocker Spaniel has been improperly fed, has been sick, or is having puppies. Vitamins and minerals are naturally present in all the foods; and to ensure against any loss through processing, they are added in concentrated form to the dog food you use. Except on the advice of your veterinarian, added amounts of vitamins can prove harmful to your Cocker Spaniel! The same risk goes with minerals.

FEEDING SCHEDULE

When and how much food to give your Cocker Spaniel? As to when (except in the instance of puppies), suit yourself. You may feed two meals per day or the same amount in one single feeding, either morning or night. As to how to prepare the food and how much to give, it is generally best to follow the directions on the

Feeding kibble between meals is an acceptable practice in nourishing your growing Cocker Spaniel puppy.

food package. Your own Cocker Spaniel may want a little more or a little less.

Fresh, cool water should always be available to your Cocker Spaniel. This is important to good health throughout his lifetime.

ALL COCKER SPANIELS NEED TO CHEW

Puppies and young Cocker Spaniels need something with resistance to chew on while their teeth and jaws are developing—for cutting the puppy teeth, to induce growth of the permanent teeth under the puppy teeth, to assist in getting rid of the puppy teeth at the proper time, to help the permanent teeth through the gums, to ensure normal jaw development, and to settle the permanent teeth solidly in the jaws.

The adult Cocker Spaniel's desire to chew stems from the instinct for tooth cleaning, gum massage, and jaw exercise—plus the need for an outlet for periodic doggie tensions.

This is why dogs, especially puppies and young dogs, will often destroy property worth hundreds of dollars when their chewing instinct is not diverted from their owner's possessions.

PHOTO BY ISABELLE FRANCAIS.

A crew of Cocker puppies can be quite a handful, and often destructive. Be sure to provide proper chew toys to satisfy their nibbling needs.

And this is why you should provide your Cocker Spaniel with something to chew— something that has the necessary functional qualities, is desirable from the Cocker Spaniel's viewpoint, and is safe for him.

It is very important that your Cocker Spaniel not be permitted to chew on anything he can break or on any indigestible thing from which he can bite sizable chunks. Sharp pieces, such as from a bone which can be broken by a dog, may pierce the intestinal wall and kill. Indigestible things that can be bitten off in chunks, such as from shoes or rubber or plastic toys, may cause an intestinal stoppage (if not regurgitated) and bring painful death, unless surgery is promptly performed.

Strong natural bones, such as 4- to 8-inch lengths of round shin

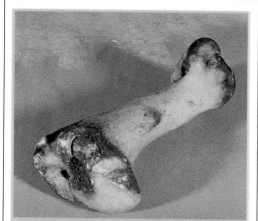

Strong natural beef bones, the kind that are available only from a butcher or a pet shop, may keep your Cocker content but are less desirable than nylon or polyurethane bones, which do not damage tooth enamel.

bone from mature beef—either the kind you can get from a butcher or one of the variety available commercially in pet stores—may serve your Cocker Spaniel's teething needs if his mouth is large enough to handle them effectively. You may be tempted to give your Cocker Spaniel puppy a smaller bone and he may not be able to break it when you do, but

Cockers have such strong jaws that most ordinary pacifiers (chew devices) are immediately destroyed. The Hercules has been designed with Cockers and other similar breeds in mind. This bone is made of polyurethane, like car bumpers.

puppies grow rapidly and the power of their jaws constantly increases until maturity. This means that a growing Cocker Spaniel may break one of the smaller bones at any time, swallow the pieces, and die painfully before you realize what is wrong.

All hard natural bones are very abrasive. If your Cocker Spaniel is an avid chewer, natural bones may wear away his teeth prematurely; hence, they then should be taken away from your dog when the teething purposes have been served. The badly worn,

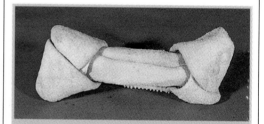

Rawhide is probably the best-selling dog chew. It can be dangerous and cause a dog to choke on it as it swells when wet. A molded, melted rawhide mixed with casein is available (though always scarce). This is the only suitable rawhide for Cocker Spaniels.

and usually painful, teeth of many mature dogs can be traced to excessive chewing on natural bones.

Contrary to popular belief, knuckle bones that can be chewed up and swallowed by your Cocker Spaniel provide little, if any, usable calcium or other nutriment. They do, however, disturb the digestion of most dogs and cause them to vomit the nourishing food they need.

Dried rawhide products of various types, shapes, sizes, and prices are available on the market and have become quite popular. However, they don't serve the primary chewing functions very well; they are a bit messy when wet from mouthing, and most Cocker Spaniels chew them up rather rapidly—but they have

PHOTO BY ISABELLE FRANCAIS.

Providing your puppy with proper teething toys will ensure happiness for both Cocker and owner.

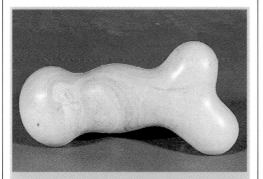

This is the Galileo Bone, the strongest chew toy in the world. The shape of this annealed, virgin-nylon bone was based on drawings and theories of Galileo Galilei, who in addition to his astronomic discoveries also did a conclusive study on the tensile strength of bones.

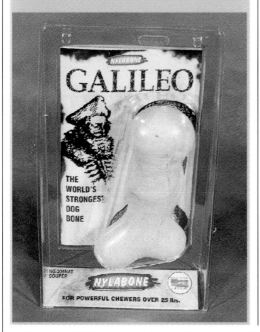

been considered safe for dogs until recently. Now, more and more incidents of death, and near death, by strangulation have been reported to be the results of partially swallowed chunks of rawhide swelling in the throat. More recently, some veterinarians have been attributing cases of acute constipation to large pieces of incompletely digested rawhide in the intestine.

A new product, molded rawhide, is very safe. During the process, the rawhide is melted and then injection molded into the familiar dog shape. It is very hard and is eagerly accepted by Cocker Spaniels. The melting process also sterilizes the rawhide. Don't confuse this with pressed rawhide, which is nothing more than small strips of rawhide squeezed together.

The nylon bones, especially those with natural meat and bone fractions added, are probably the most complete, safe, and economical answer to the chewing need. Dogs cannot break them or bite off sizable chunks; hence, they are

Nylon chewing device—before and after. When the device looks like the lower sample, it is time to buy a new one.

completely safe—and being longer lasting than other things offered for the purpose, they are economical.

Hard chewing raises little bristle-like projections on the surface of the nylon bones—to provide effective interim tooth cleaning and vigorous gum massage, much in the same way your toothbrush does it for you. The little projections are raked off and swallowed in the form of thin shavings, but the chemistry of the nylon is such that they break

The Plaque Attacker® is a therapeutic chew device specifically designed to aid in the fight against periodontal disease.

down in the stomach fluids and pass through without effect.

The toughness of the nylon provides the strong chewing resistance needed for important jaw exercise and effectively aids teething functions, but there is no tooth wear because nylon is non-abrasive. Being inert, nylon does not support the growth of microorganisms; and it can be washed in soap and water or it can be sterilized by boiling or in an autoclave.

Nylabone® is highly recommended by veterinarians as a safe, healthy nylon bone that can't splinter or chip. Nylabone® is frizzled by the dog's chewing action, creating a toothbrush-like surface that

The small-knot Pooch Pacifier is an ideal chew device to soothe the teething needs of your Cocker Spaniel puppy.

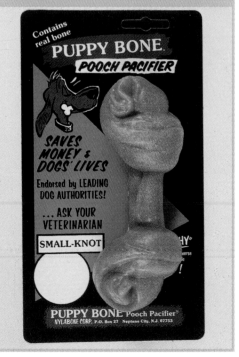

Contains real bone
PUPPY BONE.
POOCH PACIFIER
SAVES MONEY & DOGS' LIVES
Endorsed by LEADING DOG AUTHORITIES!
... ASK YOUR VETERINARIAN
SMALL-KNOT
PUPPY BONE Pooch Pacifier®
NYLABONE CORP. P.O. Box 27 Neptune City, N.J. 07753

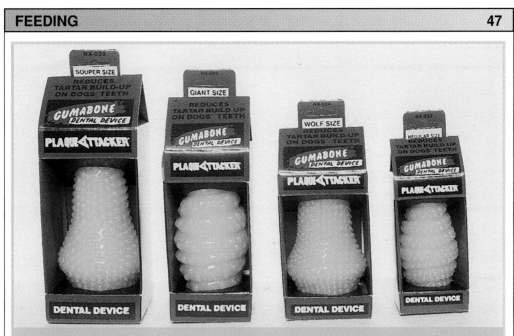

Excellent chewing devices, Plaque Attackers® have raised dental tips that actually attack the plaque and tartar build-up on your Cocker Spaniel's teeth.

cleanses the teeth and massages the gums. Nylabone®, the only chew products made of flavor-impregnated solid nylon, are available in your local pet shop. Nylabone® is superior to the cheaper bones because it is made of virgin nylon, which is the strongest and longest-lasting type of nylon available. The cheaper bones are made from recycled or re-ground nylon scraps, and have a tendency to break apart and split easily.

Nothing, however, substitutes for periodic professional attention for your Cocker Spaniel's teeth and gums, not any more than your toothbrush can do that for you. Have your Cocker Spaniel's teeth cleaned at least once a year by your veterinarian (twice a year is better) and he will be happier, healthier, and far more pleasant to live with.

A good polyurethane bone, such as this Gumabone, lasts ten times as long as a typical rawhide chew and is your best bet for the aggressive-chewing Cocker puppy.

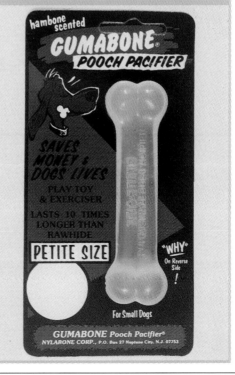

Your Cocker Spaniel deserves to be properly trained. Begin when your pet is a puppy to ensure the best results.

TRAINING

You owe proper training to your Cocker Spaniel. The right and privilege of being trained is his birthright; and whether your Cocker Spaniel is going to be a handsome, well-mannered housedog and companion, a show dog, or whatever possible use he or off lead. He must be mannerly and polite wherever he goes; he must be polite to strangers on the street and in stores. He must be mannerly in the presence of other dogs. He must not bark at children on roller skates, motorcycles, or other domestic

Training your Cocker begins with basic obedience, which can be taught with simple commands and rewards.

may be put to, the basic training is always the same—all must start with basic obedience, or what might be called "manner training."

Your Cocker Spaniel must come instantly when called and obey the "Sit" or "Down" command just as fast; he must walk quietly at "Heel," whether on animals. And he must be restrained from chasing cats. It is not a dog's inalienable right to chase cats, and he must be reprimanded for it.

PROFESSIONAL TRAINING

How do you go about this training? Well, it's a very simple

procedure, pretty well standardized by now. First, if you can afford the extra expense, you may send your Cocker Spaniel to a professional trainer, where in 30 to 60 days he will learn how to be a "good dog." If you enlist the services of a good professional trainer, follow his advice of when to come to see the dog. No, he won't forget you, but too-frequent visits at the wrong time may slow down his training progress. And using a "pro" trainer means that you will have to go for some training, too, after the trainer feels your Cocker Spaniel is ready to go home. You will have to learn how your Cocker Spaniel works, just what to expect of him and how to use what the dog has learned after he is home.

OBEDIENCE TRAINING CLASS

Another way to train your Cocker Spaniel (many experienced Cocker Spaniel people think this is the best) is to join an obedience training class right in your own community. There is such a group in nearly every community nowadays. Here you will be working with a group of people who are also just starting out. You will actually be training your own dog, since all work is done under the direction of a

Training dogs in a group teaches concentration and that commands are to be obeyed despite distractions.

head trainer who will make suggestions to you and also tell you when and how to correct your Cocker Spaniel's errors. Then, too, working with such a group, your Cocker Spaniel will learn to get along with other dogs. And, what is more important, he will learn to do exactly what he is told to do, no matter how much confusion there is around him or how great the temptation is to go his own way.

Write to your national kennel club for the location of a training club or class in your locality. Sign up. Go to it regularly—every session! Go early and leave late! Both you and your Cocker Spaniel will benefit tremendously.

TRAIN HIM BY THE BOOK

The third way of training your Cocker Spaniel is by the book. Yes, you can do it this way and do a good job of it too. But in using the book method, select a book, buy it, study it carefully; then study it some more, until the procedures are almost second nature to you. Then start your training. But stay with the book and its advice and exercises. Don't start in and then make up a few rules of your own. If you don't follow the book, you'll get into jams you can't get out of by yourself. If after a few hours of short training sessions your Cocker Spaniel is still not working as he should, get back to the book for

PHOTO BY ISABELLE FRANCAIS.

This group of unpolished puppies could prove to be a bumbling bunch without proper training.

Just Say "Good Dog" is a thorough, easy-to-understand manual outlining the most effective techniques of teaching your dog.

a study session, because it's your fault, not the dog's! The procedures of dog training have been so well systemized that it must be your fault, since literally thousands of fine Cocker Spaniels have been trained by the book.

After your Cocker Spaniel is "letter perfect" under all conditions, then, if you wish, go on to advanced training and trick work.

Your Cocker Spaniel will love his obedience training, and you'll burst with pride at the finished product! Your Cocker Spaniel will enjoy life even more, and you'll enjoy your Cocker Spaniel more. And remember—you *owe good training to your Cocker Spaniel.*

PHOTO BY ISABELLE FRANCAIS.

Cocker Spaniels need plenty of exercise and training to truly fulfill their needs and happiness.

YOUR NEW COCKER PUPPY

SELECTION

When you do pick out a Cocker Spaniel puppy as a pet, don't be hasty; the longer you study puppies, the better you will understand them. Make it your transcendent concern to select only one that radiates good health and spirit and is lively on his feet, whose eyes are bright, whose coat shines, and who comes forward eagerly to make and to cultivate your acquaintance. Don't fall for any shy little darling that wants to retreat to his bed or his box, or plays coy behind other puppies or people, or hides his head under your arm or jacket appealing to your protective instinct. *Pick the Cocker Spaniel puppy who forthrightly picks you! The feeling of attraction should be mutual!*

PHOTO BY ISABELLE FRANCAIS.

When choosing your Cocker puppy, make health, spirit, and liveliness your primary concerns.

DOCUMENTS

Now, a little paper work is in order. When you purchase a purebred Cocker Spaniel puppy, you should receive a transfer of ownership, registration material, and other "papers" (a list of the immunization shots, if any, the puppy may have been given; a note on whether or not the puppy has been wormed; a diet and feeding schedule to which the puppy is accustomed) and you are welcomed as a fellow owner to a long, pleasant association with a most lovable pet, and more (news)paper work.

GENERAL PREPARATION

You have chosen to own a particular Cocker Spaniel puppy. You have chosen it very carefully over all other breeds and all other puppies. So before you ever get that Cocker Spaniel puppy home, you will have prepared for its arrival by reading everything you can get your hands on having to do with the management of Cocker Spaniels and puppies. True, you will run into many conflicting opinions, but at least you will not be starting "blind." Read, study, digest. Talk over your plans with your veterinarian, other "Cocker Spaniel people," and the seller of your Cocker Spaniel puppy.

When you get your Cocker

Spaniel puppy, you will find that your reading and study are far from finished. You've just scratched the surface in your plan to provide the greatest possible comfort and health for your Cocker Spaniel; and, by the same token, you do want to assure yourself of the greatest possible

usually make the trip without mishap. If the pup starts to drool and to squirm, stop the car for a few minutes. Have newspapers handy in case of car-sickness. A covered carton lined with newspapers provides protection for puppy and car, if you are driving alone. Avoid excitement

PHOTO BY ROBERT PEARCY.

A litter of Cocker puppies can look exactly the same, so it is important to study their behavior. Stay away from the overly shy and overly aggressive pup: choose a puppy that's somewhere in between.

enjoyment of this wonderful creature. You must be ready for this puppy mentally as well as in the physical requirements.

TRANSPORTATION

If you take the puppy home by car, protect him from drafts, particularly in cold weather. Wrapped in a towel and carried in the arms or lap of a passenger, the Cocker Spaniel puppy will

and unnecessary handling of the puppy on arrival. A Cocker Spaniel puppy is a very small "package" to be making a complete change of surroundings and company, and he needs frequent rest and refreshment to renew his vitality.

THE FIRST DAY AND NIGHT

When your Cocker Spaniel puppy arrives in your home, put

him down on the floor and don't pick him up again, except when it is absolutely necessary. He is a dog, a real dog, and must not be lugged around like a rag doll. Handle him as little as possible, and permit no one to pick him up and baby him. To repeat, *put your Cocker Spaniel puppy on the floor or the ground and let him stay*

and sniff over his new home. If it's dark, put on the lights. Let him roam for a few minutes while you and everyone else concerned sit quietly or go about your routine business. Let the puppy come back to you.

Playmates may cause an immediate problem if the new Cocker Spaniel puppy is to be

PHOTO BY ISABELLE FRANCAIS.

Probably the easiest way to select a Cocker from a large litter is to pick the puppy that picks you.

there except when it may be necessary to do otherwise.

Quite possibly your Cocker Spaniel puppy will be afraid for a while in his new surroundings, without his mother and littermates. Comfort him and reassure him, but don't console him. Don't give him the "oh-you-poor-itsy-bitsy-puppy" treatment. Be calm, friendly, and reassuring. Encourage him to walk around

greeted by children or other pets. If not, you can skip this subject. The natural affinity between puppies and children calls for some supervision until a live-and-let-live relationship is established. This applies particularly to a Christmas puppy, when there is more excitement than usual and more chance for a puppy to swallow something upsetting. It is a better plan to welcome the puppy several days before or after the holiday week. Like a baby, your Cocker Spaniel puppy needs much rest and should not be over-handled. Once a child realizes that a puppy has "feelings" similar to his own, and can readily be hurt or injured, the opportunities for play and responsibilities provide exercise and training for both.

For his first night with you, he should be put where he is to sleep every night—say in the kitchen, since its floor can usually be easily cleaned. Let him explore the kitchen to his heart's content; close doors to confine him there. Prepare his food and feed him lightly the first night. Give him a pan with some water in it—not a lot, since most puppies will try to drink the whole pan dry. Give him an old coat or shirt to lie on. Since a coat or shirt will be strong in human scent, he will pick it out to lie on, thus furthering his feeling of security in the room where he has just been fed.

HOUSEBREAKING HELPS

Now, sooner or later—mostly sooner—your new Cocker Spaniel puppy is going to "puddle" on the floor. First take a newspaper and lay it on the puddle until the urine is soaked up onto the paper. *Save this paper.* Now take a cloth with soap and water, wipe up the

PHOTO BY ISABELLE FRANCAIS.

Closely examine a few puppies so that you can make a judgment on the overall health of the litter. Eyes should be clear and dry; the coat clean and free from fleas and other parasites, bone structure sturdy, and expression intelligent and alert.

Preparing your home for your new puppy's arrival will make the adjustment process easier for both your Cocker and your family. Photo by Isabelle Francais.

Your new Cocker Spaniel will take some time to get used to his new surroundings. Be patient and provide lots of love and understanding.

PHOTO BY ISABELLE FRANCAIS.

Sometimes the arrival of a new puppy is just what your older Cocker needs to put a little spring back into his step.

floor and dry it well. Then take the wet paper and place it on a fairly large square of newspapers in a convenient corner. When cleaning up, always keep a piece of wet paper on top of the others. Every time he wants to "squat," he will seek out this spot and use the papers. (This routine is rarely necessary for more than three days.) Now leave your Cocker Spaniel puppy for the night. Quite probably he will cry and howl a bit; some are more stubborn than others on this matter. But let him stay alone for the night. This may seem harsh treatment, but it is the best procedure in the long run. Just let him cry; he will weary of it sooner or later.

Caring for more than one Cocker Spaniel takes a little more work on the owner's part, but the dogs will appreciate the company.

SHOWING A COCKER SPANIEL

A show Cocker Spaniel is a comparatively rare thing. He is one out of several litters of puppies. He happens to be born with a degree of physical perfection that closely approximates the standard by which the breed is judged in the show ring. Such a dog should, on maturity, be able to win or approach his championship in good, fast company at the larger shows. Upon finishing his championship, he is apt to be as highly desirable as a breeding animal. As a proven stud, he will automatically command a high price for service.

Showing Cocker Spaniels is a lot of fun—yes, but it is a highly competitive sport. While all the experts were once beginners, the odds are against a novice. You will be showing against experienced handlers, often people who have devoted a lifetime to breeding, picking the right ones, and then showing those dogs through to their championships. Moreover, the most perfect Cocker Spaniel ever born has faults, and in your hands the faults will be far more evident than with the experienced handler who knows how to minimize his Cocker Spaniel's faults. These are

PHOTO BY ISABELLE FRANCAIS.

Competing in dog shows can be very exciting and is a great form of socialization for both owner and dog.

but a few points on the sad side of the picture.

The experienced handler, as I say, was not born knowing the ropes. He learned—*and so can you!* You can if you will put in the same time, study and keen observation that he did. But it will take time!

KEY TO SUCCESS

First, search for a truly fine show prospect. Take the puppy home, raise him by the book, and as carefully as you know how, give him every chance to mature into the Cocker Spaniel you hoped for. My advice is to keep your dog out of big shows, even Puppy Classes, until he is mature. Maturity in the male is roughly two years; with the female, 14 months or so. When your Cocker Spaniel is approaching maturity, start out at match shows, and, with this experience for both of you, then go gunning for the big wins at the big shows.

Next step, read the standard by which the Cocker Spaniel is judged. Study it until you know it by heart. Having done this, and while your puppy is at home (where he should be) growing into a normal, healthy Cocker Spaniel, go to every dog show you can possibly reach. Sit at the ringside and watch Cocker Spaniel judging. Keep your ears and eyes open. Do your own judging, holding each of those dogs against the standard, which you now know by heart.

In your evaluations, don't start looking for faults. Look for the virtues—the best qualities. How does a given Cocker Spaniel shape

PHOTO BY ISABELLE FRANCAIS.

If you plan to show Cocker Spaniels, go to a few dog shows to get an idea of what a good Cocker looks like. This stunning Cocker is Ch. La-Shay's Bart Simpson, the 1995 Westminster Best of Breed winner (black variety). Owners, Samuel B. and Marion W. Lawrence.

PHOTO BY ISABELLE FRANCAIS.

Ch. Rendition Triple Play, the 1995 Westminster Best of Breed winner (parti-color variety). Owner, Brigitte Berg.

up against the standard? Having looked for and noted the virtues, then note the faults and see what prevents a given Cocker Spaniel from standing correctly or moving well. Weigh these faults against the virtues, since, ideally, every feature of the dog should contribute to the harmonious whole dog.

"RINGSIDE JUDGING"

It's a good practice to make notes on each Cocker Spaniel, always holding the dog against the standard. In "ringside judging," forget your personal preference for this or that feature. What does the standard say about it? Watch carefully as the judge places the dogs in a given class. It is difficult from the ringside always to see why number one was placed over the second dog. Try to follow the judge's reasoning. Later try to talk with the judge after he is finished. Ask him questions as to why he placed certain Cocker Spaniels and not others. Listen while the judge explains his placings, and, I'll say right here, any judge worthy of his license should be able to give reasons.

When you're not at the ringside, talk with the fanciers and breeders who have Cocker Spaniels. Don't be afraid to ask opinions or say that you don't know. You have a lot of listening to do, and it will help you a great deal and speed up your personal progress if you are a good listener.

THE NATIONAL CLUB

You will find it worthwhile to join the national Cocker Spaniel club and to subscribe to its magazine. From the national club, you will learn the location of an approved regional club near you. Now, when your young Cocker Spaniel is eight to ten months old, find out the dates of match shows

1995 Westminster Best of Breed (A.S.C.O.B.) winner Ch. Glen Abbey's Jokers Wild. Owners, Mary Maloney and Lee Bergstrom.

in your section of the country. These differ from regular shows only in that no championship points are given. These shows are especially designed to launch young dogs (and new handlers) on a show career.

ENTER MATCH SHOWS

With the ring deportment you have watched at big shows firmly in mind and practice, enter your Cocker Spaniel in as many match shows as you can. When in the ring, you have two jobs. One is to see to it that your Cocker Spaniel is always being seen to its best advantage. The other job is to keep your eye on the judge to see what he may want you to do next.

Watch only the judge and your Cocker Spaniel. Be quick and be alert; do exactly as the judge directs. Don't speak to him except to answer his questions. If he does something you don't like, don't say so. And don't irritate the judge (and everybody else) by constantly talking and fussing with your dog.

In moving about the ring, remember to keep clear of dogs beside you or in front of you. It is my advice to you *not* to show your Cocker Spaniel in a regular point show until he is at least close to maturity and after both you and your dog have had time to perfect ring manners and poise in the match shows.

INDEX

Adenovirus, 35
Agility, 28
American Kennel Club, 1, 9
Anal sacs, 34
ASCOB, 15
Bathing, 19
Bones, 44
Bordetella, 35, 36
Borreliosis, 37
Brain disease, 35
Breeding, 1
Bronchitis, 36
Canned food, 40
Cataracts, 34
Cherry eyes, 33
Chewing, 43
Color, 15
Conjunctivitis, 34
Coprophagia, 36
Coronavirus, 36
Deer tick, 37
Diet, 39
Distemper, 35
Documents, 53
Dry food, 40
Encephalomyelitis, 35
English Cocker Spaniel, 2
Entropion, 34
Epilepsy, 34
Facial paralysis, 34
Glaucoma, 34
Grooming tools, 19
Gun dog, 4
Hardpad, 35
Hepatitis, 35
Hip dysplasia, 34
Housebreaking, 56
Housing, 7
Hunting, 30
Hypothyroidism, 34

Kennel, 7
Kennel Club (England), 9
Kennel cough, 35, 36
Leptospirosis, 36
Lyme disease, 37
Maturity, 62
Minerals, 41
Molded rawhide, 45
Nutrition, 40
Nylon bones, 45
Obedience, 25, 49
—classes, 51
—competition, 25
—training, 51
Obstacle course, 29
Origin, 2
Parainfluenza, 36
Parti-color, 15
Parvovirus, 35
Pneumonia, 36
Protein, 40
Rabies, 37
Red Brucie, 2
Retrieving, 31
Selection, 53
Skin problems, 34
Slicker brush, 20
Spaniels, 1
Staph dermatitis, 34
Supplements, 41
Tearing, 33
Tracheobronchitis, 35
Tracking, 26
Training class, 50
Transportation, 54
Trimming, 20
Vaccination, 35
Vitamins, 40
Von Willebrand's disease, 34
Western black-legged tick, 37